From Here to Everywhere

Written and Illustrated by
Robyn Beaufoy

Copyright © 2021 by Robyn Beaufoy.

All rights reserved. No part of this publication may be reproduced, distributed or transmitted in any form or by any means, including photocopying, recording, or other electronic or mechanical methods, without the prior written permission of the publisher, except in the case of brief quotations embodied in critical reviews and certain other noncommercial uses permitted by copyright law.

For permission requests, write to the author, at:
Waldorfish, Inc.
support@waldorfish.com

Waldorfish Press is an independent publisher of books that foster connection & warmth.

From Here to Everywhere/ Robyn Beaufoy. —1st ed.
ISBN Paperback: 978-1-7369844-0-6
ISBN Hardback: 978-1-7369844-1-3

For Mika and Iris.
Make it sweet.

My grandpa had a laugh that could fill a room.

When he started telling a story, it didn't take long before everyone else was laughing too.
I loved listening to his stories.

My grandpa taught me how to take care of his bees.

He taught me that if you're patient and you watch right at sunset, you'll see the bees swirling above their boxes, gathering the last heat from the day.

My grandpa loved his bees.

He often asked me to help him pick blackberries from along his back fence.

He had a special hat he wore just for picking berries. Sometimes, he would let me wear it.

"Your grandma makes the best blackberry pie," he used to say. My grandpa sure loved eating pie.

One winter he taught me how to ski. We swooshed down the slopes together, arms open wide, yelling, "BONZAI!"

No one knew why he liked to say that. Not even my grandpa could say for certain. He sure did love to ski, though.

He wanted to teach me how to jump out of an airplane, but my mom and grandma said I was too young. Instead, he showed me the special pants he wore when he jumped.

He said they were his good luck pants. "One of these days we'll do it! Don't you worry!" he whispered.
My grandpa loved to do things that were a little bit scary.

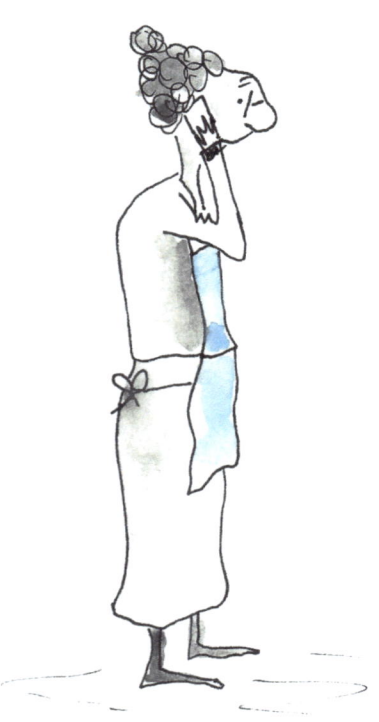

One afternoon, not too long ago, I heard my mom talking on the phone with my grandma. When they finished talking, I could see my mom was sad.

She told me my grandpa was sick. "Does he have a cold?" I asked.

She said this was a different kind of sick. The kind of sick he wouldn't get better from.

After that day, we started spending a lot of time at my grandpa's house. My grandpa spent a lot of time resting.
I would run over after school and sit in bed with him.

He showed me old pictures of himself climbing mountains, swimming with sharks, and driving race cars.

Sometimes in the evenings, my mom and grandma would sit with him. They would knit and ask him to tell them stories about when he was a boy.

I liked to stand in the doorway where no one could see me, and listen to them laughing.

My grandpa sure loved to tell stories.

A few times my grandpa was in a dark, cloudy mood.

One time I ran down to my boulder by the creek, worried that I had made him angry.

My grandma found me there. She told me that it was my grandpa's sickness that made him grumpy, not me.

Hearing that made me feel a little bit better, but also a little bit mad. Grandma said she knew just how I was feeling.

We threw rocks at the creek
till sunset that night.

Over the next few weeks, my grandpa started sleeping more and more.

He often wasn't awake when I came over after school. I sat with him anyway, reading some of his favorite books out loud.

My grandma said he knew I was there.
She said he appreciated my company.

One afternoon while we were pulling weeds in the garden, I asked my grandma if we would still be able to spend time with Grandpa after he died. "Oh yes!" she said. "Not in the same way we do now, but yes, you'll see."

I wondered where he was going. Where would he be after he died? "Everywhere." My grandma told me. "Grandpa will be everywhere."

And you know what?
She was right.

This summer I could feel my grandpa with me every time I watched his bees swirling above their boxes at sunset.

In the fall, he was with us every time we ate one of grandma's blackberry pies. I made sure to wear his special hat whenever I picked the berries.

This winter I know my grandpa was smiling when my mom and I skied down the slopes together, arms open wide, yelling, "BONZAI!"

And I know he'll be with my grandma and me this spring when we learn how to jump out of an airplane.

I'm a little bit scared, so Grandma says I should be the one to wear his good luck pants.

ADDITIONAL RESOURCES

For a deeper exploration, head to www.waldorfish.com/fhte/bonus. There you will find a beautiful downloadable worksheet that your family can use to brainstorm ideas for honoring & celebrating the legacy of friends and loved ones.

Hospice Foundation of America
Grief is a reaction to loss. Our reactions are unique and individual; none of us experiences grief exactly the same way. HFA will connect your family to local support groups and resources. https://hospicefoundation.org/Grief-(1)

ABOUT THE AUTHOR

Robyn Beaufoy is a Canadian-born artist, educator, and parent (to both teens and cats). She co-founded Waldorfish.com, an online resource for educators and families interested in Rudolf Steiner's Waldorf method of learning and human development.

She splits her time between the virtual world and the very tangible soil of her vegetable garden, toiling vigorously and finding joy and meaning in both endeavors. Thousands of followers have found a community of like-minded thinkers and doers in Waldorfish.

When not in the garden, Robyn can be found painting, baking, brewing kombucha from scratch, and feeding her (always hungry) children.

www.ingramcontent.com/pod-product-compliance
Lightning Source LLC
Chambersburg PA
CBHW042257100526
44589CB00003B/56